MOOSEY
SAVES MONEY

Written by Michael J. Pellowski
Illustrated by Paul Harvey

Troll Associates

Library of Congress Cataloging in Publication Data

Pellowski, Michael.
  Moosey saves money.

  Summary: Moosey loves to save money but finally
learns that there are times when money has to be
spent.
  [1. Moose—Fiction. 2. Money—Fiction] I. Harvey,
Paul, 1926-   ill. II. Title.
PZ7.P3656Mo   1986   [E]   85-14053
ISBN 0-8167-0628-X (lib. bdg.)
ISBN 0-8167-0629-8 (pbk.)

10   9   8   7   6   5   4   3

MOOSEY
SAVES MONEY

Moosey was a little moose.
He was a quiet, little moose.
He did not like to spend money.
Moosey liked to save money.

Saving money is good. Money is
good to have. But sometimes
you must spend. Did Moosey
spend? No! He saved and saved!

Moosey did not like things to
cost a lot. His house did not cost
a lot. It was a quiet, little
house. Moosey liked it that way.

A house that does not cost a lot
needs fixing. Fixing things costs
money. How did Moosey save
money? He fixed things himself.
But Moosey was not good at
fixing things.

8

"A quiet house is a good house,"
said Moosey.
Moosey sat down. He sat down
in his quiet, little house. Then
the quiet stopped. A little noise
started.

Drip!
Drip! Drop!
Drip! Drippity drip!
"What is that?" called Moosey.

10

Drip! Drop! Drip!
"What is that noise?" said the
moose. "I do not like noise. I
like a quiet house. Stop that
dripping!"

Did the dripping stop? Oh no! It dripped and dropped and dripped.

"That drip needs fixing," said Moosey.

Drip! Drop! Drip!
Moosey looked for the drip.
Drippity drip!
Moosey found the drip. His sink
was dripping water. What a bad
drip it was!

13

Moosey looked at the sink.
"That noise must stop," he said.
"That drip must be fixed. I will
call Fix-It Fox."

Moosey called.
"I need someone to fix a drippy
sink," he said.
Fix-It Fox said, "I will look at
the drip."

Fix-It Fox went to Moosey's
house. He looked at the sink. He
looked at the drip. He looked
and looked.
"It will cost ten dollars to fix,"
he said.

"Ten dollars!" yelled Moosey.
"Ten dollars to stop water
dripping! Ten dollars is a lot of
money. Spend ten dollars to fix
a drip? Oh no! I will fix it
myself and save money."

Fix-It Fox looked at Moosey.
"It is a bad drip," said Fix-It
Fox. "It is not easy to fix.
Sometimes you have to spend
money. You cannot always save
by fixing things yourself."

18

"Fixing a drippy sink is easy,"
said Moosey. "I am good at
fixing things."
Fix-It Fox went away.

Drip! Drop! Drip!
The drip got noisier.
"A hammer is what I need,"
said Moosey. "A hammer will fix
my sink. It will stop the water
from dripping."

20

Moosey got a hammer.
"I will tap the sink with a
hammer," he said. "Ten easy
taps will stop the water from
dripping."

Drip!
Tap! Tap!
Drip! Drop!
Tap! Tap! Tap!
Moosey said, "Five more taps
will fix it."

Tap!

"OUCH!" yelled Moosey. The hammer did not tap the sink. It tapped Moosey's thumb.

"Ouch! Ouch! Ouch!" Moosey yelled. "I hammered my thumb!"

Moosey looked at his thumb.
It looked bad.
"My thumb needs a doctor,"
said Moosey. "I cannot fix a
hammered thumb myself. I will
go to Doctor Duck."
Moosey went to Doctor Duck's
house. He sat down. Doctor
Duck looked at Moosey.
"What needs fixing?" the doctor
said.

"I hammered my thumb," said
Moosey.
Doctor Duck looked at Moosey's
thumb.
"How did you do it?" he asked.
Moosey said, "I was tapping my
drippy sink."

"A drippy sink is not easy to fix," said Doctor Duck.
He fixed Moosey's hammered thumb. Fixing the thumb cost Moosey five dollars.
"Fix-It Fox fixes noisy drips," said the doctor. "Call him."

"I do not like to spend money,"
said the moose. "Fix-It Fox will
charge me ten dollars. I will
quiet that noisy drip myself."
He went back to his house.

Drip! Drippity drip!
The drip was noisier now.
"I will fix you," Moosey said to
the sink. "I will not hammer my
thumb this time."
Moosey started to tap the sink.
Then a drip dropped on his
hammer. The drop of water
made the hammer slippery.
It slipped. It dropped. It
dropped on Moosey's toe.

"OH! OH! OH!" yelled Moosey.
"My toe! Oh, you bad, bad
drip! Ouch! Ouch! Ouch!"
Back to Doctor Duck went
Moosey.
"What needs fixing now?" said
Doctor Duck. He looked at
Moosey.

30

Moosey said, "I dropped a
hammer on my toe."
"Oh no," said Doctor Duck.
He looked at Moosey's toe.
"It is not bad," he said. "I can
fix it easily."
The toe cost five dollars to fix.

Moosey went home. Was his
little house quiet? No!
The drip was dripping.
Drip! Drop! Drip!

The drip was bad. Water
dropped from the sink. Water,
water dripping everywhere!
The hammer was in water.

Water is slippery. Moosey went
to get the hammer. He slipped.
Down he went.
"Ouch oh!" yelled Moosey.
"My back needs fixing now."

Moosey did not go to the doctor.
He called Doctor Duck. Doctor
Duck went to Moosey's little
house.

"I will look at your back," said
Doctor Duck.
He looked and looked. He
tapped Moosey's back. The
doctor looked and tapped and
tapped and looked.

"Moosey," said the doctor, "your back is not bad. It does not need fixing. But you must go easy. You must sit down."

Doctor Duck started to go.
"How much will this cost?" said
Moosey.
"This will cost ten dollars," said
the doctor.
Doctor Duck went.

Moosey sat down. He wanted
quiet. Quiet is good for a
hammered thumb. Quiet is good
for a bad toe. But Moosey's
house was not quiet.
Drip! Drop! Drip!

"What a bad fix," said Moosey.
"Five dollars for a hammered
thumb. Five dollars for a bad
toe. Ten dollars for a back that
does not need fixing. I am
spending more than I am
saving."

Drip! Drop! Drip!
Moosey looked at the drippy
sink.
"Sometimes," said Moosey, "you
have to spend money. You
cannot always save by fixing
things yourself."

Moosey called Fix-It Fox. Fix-It
Fox went to Moosey's house.

Drip! Drippity drop!
"I will fix that noisy sink," the
fox said. "I will stop the water
from dripping. I am good at
fixing things."

Drip! Drop! Drip!
The fox fixed the sink.
Drip! Drop!
The water stopped.
"It stopped dripping," Moosey
yelled.

44

Moosey sat. He looked at Fix-It
Fox. What a good fixer he was!

"I fixed it," said Fix-It Fox.
"That will be ten dollars."
Said Moosey, "It is good to
spend money for a fixed sink."

46

Fix-It Fox went. The drip was
fixed.
"Good," said Moosey. "No more
water drops. No more drippy
sinks. No more noise."

Moosey sat in his quiet, little house.

"Saving money is good," said Moosey. "But when you have to spend money, spend it."